What's was your first response when you read the title of this book? The word *judgment* provokes so many emotions, thoughts, and ideas. In its most simple definition, God's judgment is His active making of wrong things right. When God judges, He removes all the things that hinder love in our hearts, in our churches, so that He can have greater intimacy and compatibility with us. He longs for greater intimacy with you, and therefore His love will first confront things in us so that He can have His inheritance—a Bride fully in love and fully in unity with His heart and leadership. In this book, you will encounter the jealousy of God in removing *everything* in us, in the Church, in its leaders, so that He can fully manifest His glory and power. Judgment begins in the house of God, and I believe God is doing this in the Church today so that we can fully partner with all that God is doing in the coming days.

COREY RUSSELL
International speaker and author

In every generation God raises up prophetic voices that will speak to His people with an uncompromising boldness. I believe Jeremiah Johnson is one of the clearest and strongest in our generation. In an era defined by political correctness and tongue-tied church leaders, Jeremiah's writings are a breath of fresh air—raw truth and from a burning heart. In his newest book, *Judgment on the House of God*, the cutting edge that characterizes his ministry has never been sharper. I highly recommend Jeremiah Johnson, his ministry, and this book.

EVANGELIST DANIEL KOLENDA
President/CEO Christ for all Nations

A scalpel may be a useful tool in the hands of a surgeon; however, a scalpel is powerless when it comes to breaking an ice flow that is blocking the way of navigating a frozen river, lake, or ocean. Jeremiah Johnson has been raised up by God to break through the hard, frigid conditions so widespread throughout the Body of Christ.

I knew who Jeremiah was from a distance but having the privilege of working with him for the past six months has given me a whole new perspective of who he is in God. His writings are a written expression of his heart's longing. God is more important to him than ministry—a rare commodity these days. What you are about to read was birthed from his times of intimacy with God. His message is *His* message. Like Elijah who first stood in the presence of God before confronting Ahab, Jeremiah also speaks and writes what God reveals to him in the secret place of His presence.

I feel honored to recommend this latest book to you and I know you will be greatly blessed, but more importantly, changed.

DAVID RAVENHILL
Author and teacher

# JUDGMENT
## ON THE
# HOUSE OF GOD

## OTHER BOOKS BY JEREMIAH JOHNSON

*I See a New Prophetic Generation*

*I See a New Apostolic Generation*

*The Micaiah Company*

*Cleansing and Igniting the Prophetic*

*Cleansing and Igniting the Prophetic Study Guide*

*Trump, 2019 & Beyond*

*The Power of Consecration*

*Trump and the Future of America*

# JUDGMENT
## ON THE
## HOUSE OF GOD:

# Cleansing

# &

# Glory

## ARE

# Coming

# JEREMIAH JOHNSON

DESTINY IMAGE® PUBLISHERS, INC.
P.O. Box 310, Shippensburg, PA 17257-0310
*"Promoting Inspired Lives."*

This book and all other Destiny Image and Destiny Image Fiction books are available at Christian bookstores and distributors worldwide.

For more information on foreign distributors, call 717-532-3040.
Reach us on the Internet: www.destinyimage.com.

Cover designed by Esther Eunjoo Jun

ISBN 13 TP: 978-0-7684-5477-2
ISBN 13 eBook: 978-0-7684-5478-9
ISBN 13 HC: 978-0-7684-5480-2
ISBN 13 LP: 978-0-7684-5479-6

For Worldwide Distribution, Printed in the U.S.A.
1 2 3 4 5 6 7 8 / 24 23 22 21 20

# DEDICATION

To my beloved wife Morgan and our four children—
may we always seek a greater cleansing together as a
family so that the glory of God might truly be demon-
strated through all that we say and do. I love the five of
you with all of my heart!

# CONTENTS

# FOREWORD

*by Patricia King*

*L*et me tell you a story that I believe will reveal some of the prophetic elements found in this book.

I was married at twenty years of age and within eighteen months gave birth to our first son. In the next eighteen months our second son was born. My husband and I both worked full time in our careers, and due to many other weekly commitments life was busy for our family.

We were blessed to live in a lovely home but due to the hectic lifestyle often specific housekeeping tasks were neglected for periods—especially dusting and mopping behind and underneath furniture (after all, who's going to see it?).

One specific week I had been particularly busy and household duties were neglected. I thought I would rectify the problem by taking my entire day off the following week and engaging in a deep-cleaning of the house. My intensions were good but urgent items appeared on my schedule and to-do list and once again the housecleaning was neglected. The more I procrastinated, the more the house was infested with unwanted disarray and chaos. I had dirty dishes stacked up in the sink, expired items were growing mold in the fridge, dirty laundry everywhere, dust covered everything, and the windows were smeared with peanut butter, jam, and nose excrements from my adorable toddlers who pressed up against the windows and sliding-glass doors with their beautiful little faces and creative fingers.

I love a clean and orderly house, but I was in trouble! Every day, I was more and more uncomfortable with the mess and thought, "I really need to do something about this." It was detestable to me but I kept pushing the cleaning assignment down the list. The house unfortunately didn't clean itself but continued to decline into a greater mess than ever. You wouldn't think that a dirty house could deeply vex your soul but it sure did mine. Even when I went to bed at night, I would feel anxious about the condition of my house.

To my horror, one day my mother paid a surprise visit. As she came unannounced through the doorway, she immediately noticed the mess my home was in (actually you couldn't miss it). She looked shocked and gave me the look, like, "So what happened here?" She didn't need to say a thing, her expression delivered the assessment (or "judgment"): your house is filthy! The judgment was true, but of course I made excuses and told her how busy I had been. She just listened and quietly looked around at everything in disarray.

She finally broke the silence and said, "Well let's go to work. Where's your cleaning supplies?" She did not condemn or shame me. She assessed and then helped me clean up the mess—all of it! We actually enjoyed each other's company as we put our hands to the assignment. After many long hours, the house was back in order and clean as a whistle, just the way I like it, and just the way she trained me growing up. It felt so good—so fresh!

This gives us a great picture of how our God wants to clean His house. We were created for purity and righteousness. Everything in us longs for His divine order to be made manifest in our lives. God is going to help us to get our "house" (lives) in order and sparkly clean.

A great move of alignment and cleansing for our lives and the Church is at hand and as we lean into God's wonderful love for us. As this cleansing takes place, we will be positioned for the most powerful outpouring of the Spirit in church history. I can hardly wait. We are going to partner with God to bring cleansing and purity back into its rightful place in our lives, in His Church, and in the world—we were made for this! We will not be alone in the process as He will be right there to walk with everyone who humbles themselves and leans into His dealings. We must not let the mess remain another day.

The doctrine of judgment is significant in both the Old and New Testament. The Greek words for judge and judgment in the New Testament are *krino* and *krisis*; most often they are used in the context of separating, discerning, and to decide right or wrong. New Testament judgment is full of hope, love, and redemption as we are called into glorious holy separation unto God's heart, ways, and purposes. I love the judgments of God! Remember though that when God addresses issues with His judgments, He does not compromise or waver in His intent. He is merciful and kind but He means business.

In the example of my mother showing up in the midst of my housekeeping disaster, her assessment was accurate. The house was a mess and it had to be dealt with. As a result, we went to work to bring the home back into order—it felt so good! So does judgment when we allow it to bring us into alignment.

God loves you. It is not His heart to beat you up. He wants you safe, secure, and happy in His presence. When we are out of alignment with Him and His holy ways, we will suffer the consequences, but when we are back in order, glorious things result. Divine glory comes when divine order is in place.

God is currently emphasizing the alignment of our hearts to Him through exposure of sin, repentance, and judgment. It is a good thing—it is glorious—it needs to be embraced. In this season there will be little to no toleration of continued, intentional sin. It is time to deal with it. If we don't there will be consequences to endure. God will never withdraw His love from us, but our life in the Kingdom is on His terms.

Jeremiah Johnson is a prophet who is carrying a message to the Church—it's time to clean the house. *Judgment on the House of God: Cleansing and Glory Are Coming* is a serious and timely prophetic word. Read it with redemptive vision. Pray through it. Allow the Holy Spirit to speak to you, and respond to everything God reveals.

You are being positioned for something so glorious in God—this is the time to yield to both cleansing and glory.

# SPECIAL INTRODUCTION

*By Dr. Michael Brown*

*T*his book is not for the faint of heart or the complacent. It is certainly not for the compromised or the carnal. But it is absolutely a book for those who love God more than this world, for those who are jealous for His glory and His reputation, for those who are committed to seeing a fresh visitation of the Holy Spirit, whatever the cost or consequence. For such readers, this book is a treasure. It will bring to your knees in prayer and repentance, and it will fill you with hope for the future.

My own heart was stirred as I read, especially the chapter on addiction to ministry, which will be very important for fellow leaders. It reminded me of an entry I made in my own journal back in 1994 while praying one morning before speaking in New York City at Times Square Church:

> *DEEPEN AND EMPHASIZE QUALITY!* Too much time working for God, not enough time waiting on God; too much time attending to His business, not enough time adoring His beauty. I'm productive, but not planted; reviving others but not resting myself. As opposed to Wesley, I am too often both in haste and in a hurry. Help me, Lord, to learn what he so well learned! Thank God for faxes and modems and E-mail; but, oh, for the quiet, contemplative life that is still before the Lord (Psalm 131), that meets with Him for fresh fire, fresh marching orders, fresh manna.

Of course, we've come a long way from just faxes and modems, with a litany of endless online distractions today. But the temptations and problems remain the same—we make ministry into an idol. We gauge success by outward results and numbers more than by transformed lives. More dangerously, we mistake the adrenaline of ministry for the quality of intimacy, putting work before worship and productivity before prayer. It's a temptation I fight on a regular basis, and Jeremiah is candid about his struggles here too. May we find lasting deliverance from this destructive addiction!

This, however, is just part of the focus of this important book, as the title indicates. The emphasis is on divine judgment, beginning with the house of God. This speaks of the Lord coming as a refiner's fire that we might shine more brightly, of the Lord pruning His people that we might bear more fruit. It also reminds us that God is a righteous Judge, that He still pours out His wrath on a sinning and rebellious world, and that He lovingly rebukes His own children so that we will not be condemned with the ungodly. That is the Father's heart!

It is a terrible shame that, today, there are Christian leaders who say that there is no judgment in this age, that all of God's wrath was poured out on the cross and so there is no wrath in this era, and that no matter what we say or do as God's children, He is always happy with us. That is not the gospel, and that is not the message of Jesus. That's why He said in Revelation 3:19, speaking by the Spirit (see 3:22), "As many as I love, I rebuke and discipline. Therefore be zealous and repent" (NKJV). And that's why Paul warned repeatedly about the coming wrath—another subject we hardly hear anything about these days—urging us to live godly and upright lives today in light of what is coming on the disobedient tomorrow.

But this is not a depressing, gloom and doom message, nor is this a depressing, gloom and doom book. Instead, this is a book that carries a promise of revival, a book that is written to prepare us for a holy visitation, a book designed to make us fit and worthy carriers of the Spirit of the Lord.

May the Lord ignite a fresh hunger and thirst in your own life as you read this concise and powerful message. And may we see the revival we all long to see. Lord, light a fresh fire in us!

*Chapter One*

## AN ANGELIC VISITATION

*A*t the end of December 2018, I spoke at a prophetic conference with John and Carol Arnott,
Daniel Kolenda, and several other trusted leaders in the
charismatic movement. We were invited to share about
what we saw God doing in the body of Christ at large.
Upon arrival, I headed straight for bed so I could get
some rest and prepare for the days of ministry ahead.

As I lay in a deep sleep, two angels came and visited
me in my hotel room. One angel had fiery blue eyes
and held a huge broom in his hands. I instantly knew
him to be an angel of cleansing. The other was an angel
of glory clothed in breathtakingly beautiful garments.
Many of the colors in these garments I have no name
for. I have never seen these colors here on earth.

The angel of cleansing spoke first. If the Church
was going to be visited by the angel of glory, she must
first receive the angel of cleansing. In other words, the
visitation of the second angel was contingent upon the
Church's reception of the visitation of the first.

When I asked what that meant, the angel of cleansing responded and said, "God will *not* fill His house
with His glory until His house receives the cleansing
and purification He desires to bring."

"Too many are chasing the glory and they will
never see it," the angel continued, "for the lack of the

demonstration of glory in the Church is a direct result of the lack of consecration. Watch, for many will cry out for glory and never see it because they refuse to consecrate themselves to the Holy One of Israel. However, also watch for the remnant who will consecrate themselves and seek the face of God like never before. When and where the visitation of the cleansing is received, it is a sign to you that the glory will come. Remember, the fear of the Lord is the beginning of wisdom. Read Ezekiel 44."

Then the two angels immediately vanished from my room.

## THE BROOM AND UPPER ROOM

After sleeping the rest of the night, I awoke the following morning with the tangible presence of God filling my room. I immediately recognized that this encounter was setting the trajectory of my life and ministry for the years ahead.

I asked God specifically about the large broom that was in the hands of the angel of cleansing. And He replied.

"Jeremiah," He said, "there is a boom that is coming again to the Upper Room, but first there must be a sweeping of the broom in My house once again."

Immediately, a great expectancy and sobriety filled me. The Great Glory and Upper Room encounters of Acts 2 were clearly going to mark God's Church in the days ahead, but it would be preceded by a deep cleansing, a purification, a sweeping of the broom of cleansing. The Church must be prepared to receive and respond to this cleansing.

## Carol Arnott's Dream

The next day I had the opportunity to share my angelic encounter with Carol Arnott. To my surprise, she had received a very similar visitation several years earlier that had drastically marked her life.

In her dream, as she stood in front of the church, a whirlwind caught her up to the ceiling of the building. As God brought her back down to the floor, something like a heavy cloak was placed upon her and God gave her a word for the people, saying, "There's another cloud—a cloud of holiness. It will not be a cloud of outward, good behavior holiness, but it will be a cloud of My holiness—the reverent fear of the Lord, which is the beginning of wisdom."

According to Carol, a remarkable outpouring of grace has been happening in the Church at large over the last twenty years or so. However, some have taken that grace for granted. In her dream, the Lord had continued to speak to her: "When this holiness glory cloud comes down, when the next wave hits, My Church better have their heart right. It's time to get right with Me. Stop playing with sin and excusing it!"

As the cloud began to come down on the Church, she exclaimed in her dream, "The altar of mercy has opened. For those who want to get their hearts right, repentance is available at the altar. For those who still want to play the game of 'God Won't Mind If I Sin!'—run! Get out of here!"

"I feared for their very lives," she explained to me.

I was rocked to the core. To encounter her the morning after the angels had visited me and hear the description of her dream underscored the importance of this tremendous promise being given to the Church. There will be a true, last-days outpouring of the glory of God like never before, but *first* there must be repentance, cleansing, purification, and judgment.

The Lord reminded of the last thing the cleansing angel had told me in my dream: "Read Ezekiel 44."

Some hidden revelation and the keys to what God wanted to unveil to His Church must be there. I was determined to discover them—no matter the cost.

*Chapter Two*

## THE SONS OF ZADOCK

*I*n the quiet of my office, I sat down and began reading Ezekiel 44. The prophet, having previously finished his account of the temple, proceeds in Chapter 44 to share God's concern over what is taking place in His sanctuary. He is upset with the Levites, the priests (leadership) responsible for overseeing the house of God.

In verses six and seven, God says, "Enough of all your abominations, O house of Israel, when you brought in foreigners uncircumcised in heart...to be in My sanctuary and to profane it, even in My house." Immediately I understood the context of the cleansing angel's words.

The cleansing is coming to the priesthood first—the leadership of God's Church.

The Levites had allowed foreigners to come into the sanctuary of God. These were unfaithful and unauthorized priests and, as such, were an abomination to God. Yahweh repeats His objection to the Levites in verse eight: "And you have not kept charge of My holy things yourselves, but you have set foreigners to keep charge of My sanctuary."

## FOREIGNERS LEADING WORSHIP

As I read Ezekiel 44, I was overcome with grief. God is saying the exact same thing to the church leadership of the twenty-first century: "You have invited and welcomed individuals into My house to lead and minister who are not circumcised in heart!"

The Lord recalled to my memory an incident that had happened several years ago. I had been invited to observe the services of a large church. The pastor wanted me to spend a day with his church and then share with him any prophetic insights the Lord may have given me.

I sat through their five Sunday services and met with him afterward.

"Jeremiah," he asked, "what do you think about what you witnessed today?"

"Sir, to be honest with you," I began, "in terms of excellence, I do not believe your worship team missed one note and your sermons were as polished as I have ever heard. However, there was no real tangible glory of God that marked any of what was done today."

He was flabbergasted.

I looked at him and asked, "Do you know if any of the members of the worship band up on stage are even saved? They looked and sounded like professionals to me."

"They are the finest musicians we could hire," he responded, "and we pay each one of them 500 dollars every Sunday to play for our services."

"Okay," I agreed, aware I was on sensitive ground, "but have you ever asked if they are saved and have had a life-changing encounter with Jesus Christ? Do you know that they are not actively living in sin?"

The pastor stared at me.

I continued: "So if they are not saved, whose presence exactly are they leading the congregation into every Sunday? Sir, you have brought foreigners into the house of God who are not circumcised in heart. God is not pleased with your actions and you need to repent."

He showed me the door and asked me never to return.

# ENTERTAINMENT CHURCH

Francis Chan speaks to what he describes as an "entertainment spirit" that has overtaken parts of the house of God. According to Chan, "The benchmark of success in church services has become more about attendance than the movement of the Holy Spirit. The 'entertainment' model of church was largely adopted in the 1980s and '90s, and while it alleviated some of our boredom for a couple of hours a week, it filled our churches with self-focused consumers rather than self-sacrificing servants attuned to the Holy Spirit."[1]

The house of God was never created to become a subculture for the world where sinners lead and minister from the stage. The mission of the church is not to entertain, which seemed to be the goal of the church whose services I was asked to observe. The mandate of the Church is to make disciples and impact the culture around them with the uncompromised gospel of Jesus Christ.

## MINISTRY TO PEOPLE

In verse ten, Ezekiel prophesies concerning this leadership, warning that "the Levites who went far from Me...after their idols, shall bear the punishment for their iniquity."

In other words, Ezekiel is prophesying the judgment of God upon the leadership. But verse eleven is also confusing. "Yet they shall be ministers in My sanctuary," the Lord tells Ezekiel, "having oversight at the gates of the house and ministering in the house; they shall slaughter the burnt offering and the sacrifice for the people, and they shall stand before them to minister to them."

It's important that we stop here and digest exactly what God is saying through the prophet Ezekiel so that we can understand clearly what God is saying to the Church right now. God said through Ezekiel that the Levites would be punished for their iniquity (judged) yet they would still be given oversight of His house, having His permission to stand before the people and minister to them.

# JUDGMENT ON THE HOUSE OF GOD

I grew up hearing stories about the account of Ananias and Sapphira in Acts 5. This husband and wife were struck dead for lying to the Holy Spirit. This story (and others) contributed to a theology concerning the judgment of God. When Judgment comes, or so I and many others in the Church thought, people would die, plagues would break out, or natural disasters would take place, and through these, God's Judgment of a city (like Sodom and Gomorrah) or person (like Ananias and Sapphira) would manifest. Everyone would recognize the bowl of judgment from the book of Revelation.

After reading Ezekiel 44 at the invitation of the cleansing angel, this theology concerning the judgment of God was shifted in my thinking. I realized with shock that judgment is on the house of God right now!

"Judgment is on the house of God and many of the saints and leaders do not even recognize it!" I cried out to myself. "We are looking for some outward destruction to take place concerning the wickedness going on in the Church, and we are totally blinded to the truth of what God is doing right now!"

The judgment that God released upon the Levites (that is, the leadership) in the days of Ezekiel is that, while they continued in ministry with His permission, the *only* kind of ministry possible for them was that of *horizontal ministry!* God's judgment on the house of Israel was a limitation and restraint that allowed the Levites access only to people when they ministered. *They did not have access to God, so they could not minister to Him!*

In verses thirteen and fourteen God continues His pronouncement of Judgment: "And they shall not come near to Me to serve as a priest to Me, nor come near to any of My holy things, to the things that are most holy; but they will bear their shame and their abominations which they have committed. Yet I will appoint them to keep charge of the house, of all its service, and of all that shall be done in it."

The prophet Ezekiel is clearly revealing the presence of two types of ministry in the House of God: ministry to people and ministry to God. One is horizontal, the other vertical. God spoke to me and said, "Jeremiah, the judgment that is on My house is horizontal ministry. For the leaders may prophesy, work miracles, speak in tongues, worship, and minister to one another, but very few in this hour are actually ministering to Me. This is why I am bringing a cleansing, a deep repentance, a restored fear of who I am. For My people have become drunk on ministering to one another and forgotten about the Holy One of Israel."

# THE SONS OF ZADOK

In the midst of Ezekiel's prophetic pronouncement of judgment on the house of Israel regarding horizontal ministry, he shifts attention to the sons of Zadok and releases an incredible description of these men who valued ministry to God over ministry to people.

"But the Levitical priests, the sons of Zadok," declares the Lord, "who kept charge of My sanctuary when the sons of Israel went astray from Me, shall come near to Me to minister to Me; and they shall stand before Me to offer Me the fat and blood" (Ezek. 44:15).

Notice how the Levites in verses ten through fourteen were to "bear the punishment for their iniquity" by being restricted and limited to horizontal ministry where "they shall stand before them [that is, the people] to minister to them [the people]." But the sons of Zadok in verse fifteen are to "come near to Me to minister to Me." The Lord's original call and charge to the Levites in Numbers 18:7 was clear: "But you and your sons with you shall attend to your priesthood for everything concerning the *altar* and inside the *veil*, and you are to perform service."

The sons of Zadok, because of their commitment to God in the midst of a culture of compromise, were granted permission to minister at the altar of the Lord and go beyond the veil.

Is not this same vision and description valid for much of the Church today?

Are there not those who have made horizontal ministry to people their number-one priority in life and ministry? And are there not also those who have made vertical ministry to God their number-one priority and ministry?

The judgment of God is upon His house where horizontal ministry has become the defining desire and focus of the leadership. Where entertainment and idolatry with people abound, the judgment of God will also. However, the blessing and covenant of God remains with those who, like the sons of Zadok, understand and pursue ministry to God as their primary obligation and desire. God is calling His Church and leaders back to a place of fresh intimacy with Him, but before we can access that place we must address a type of addiction that hardly anyone in the church currently wants to talk about—ministry addiction.

# NOTE

1. Francis Chan, *Forgotten God: Reversing Our Tragic Neglect of the Holy Spirit*, (Colorado Springs, CO: David C. Cook, 2009), 15-16.

*Chapter Three*

# EXPOSING MINISTRY ADDICTION

While in full-time ministry in April of 2015, pastoring locally and traveling nationwide, I had a life-changing encounter with the Lord Jesus, who told me that He would be sitting me down, and I would not be praying, prophesying, or preaching for four months. Confused, I asked the Lord what I did wrong. He replied immediately, telling me that He was doing this because He extravagantly loved me. This kind of encounter with the Lord has happened to me on three additional occasions since 2015 at widely varying times.

## DELIVERANCE FROM MINISTRY

In 2015, two months into my "being seated," I found myself in the back of our prayer room at Heart of the Father in Lakeland, Florida, bored and frustrated. In that moment, the Holy Spirit said to me, "Do you know what your problem is?"

I was silent.

He said, "You need deliverance from ministry."

"What are You talking about, God?" I replied. "I grew up a pastor's son. I have a Bible degree. I've planted a growing church, and I travel all over the world ministering prophetically."

"Exactly," the Holy Spirit agreed. "That is exactly what I'm talking about, Jeremiah. You need deliverance from ministry!"

For the next two months, I wept on that floor over and over again as God peeled back all the layers of deception in my life—focusing on platforms, microphones, networking, speaking engagements, growing a church, meeting the needs of people, and so much more! All of it was horizontal ministry. Again and again God spoke to me during that season, saying, "I'm delivering you from ministry and setting your feet upon the sea of glass (Rev. 4). It's time to gaze upon the beauty of My Son Jesus and value the secret place far above any public place. You must learn how to treasure the prayer room far above any platform."

From that day until this very hour, God continues to deliver me from "ministry." I take planned, frequent breaks from scheduled ministry to evaluate and check my own heart concerning this issue. Out of the revelation of my own deception and blindness, my heart cries out for a generation of preachers now being prepared to completely focus on horizontal ministry—the very priority God wants to deliver us from!

The truth is that we will never recognize the strength of our bondage to horizontal ministry until we take a seat. I strongly urge ministers to disconnect from all horizontal ministry at least one month per year to make sure they are not getting their worth, value, and significance from that ministry. Our true value and significance do not come from horizontal ministry!

# MINISTRY CRACK COCAINE ADDICTION

One of the truths that God established in me during that season of encounter and sitting at His feet was that pursuing ministry opportunity and following Jesus Christ are not the same thing. Applause, platforms, microphones, and ministry connections and networking are as addicting as crack cocaine. The pursuit of horizontal ministry often serves as the cover of a dysfunctional marriage, family, and personal life. It allows many leaders to hide their heart issues because they measure God's approval by doors opening to preaching engagements rather than by their obedience to Him, their character and integrity, or the love and respect they have from their families.

We must understand that God's priority is on changing us from the inside (our character) rather than on using us on the outside (ministry).

The degree to which we agree with this statement is measured by the time we spend in the prayer room (with the sons of Zadok) and not by the time we spend on a platform. If we daydream of speaking before the masses instead of standing on the sea of glass and gazing at the beauty of Jesus Christ, our priorities are skewed and we are more than likely addicted to ministry. Oh! how I wish I had been taught about character, the secret place, and developing a healthy family and marriage while I earned my Bible degree! Instead, I was instructed on how to network, market, build a ministry platform, and please people.

It's time for a generation of ministers to demonstrate the character that matches the anointing on their lives. This fruit can only be forged in the fires of prayer and secret place devotion to Jesus Christ.

God is not interested in who we know and what doors we walk through in ministry. He wants to know if we are fasting, praying, loving our enemies, giving to the poor, and loving our spouses and children. For all the major addictions being addressed in the church today, why is ministry addiction never discussed or exposed?

We must seek deep cleansing and repentance in this area if we are to experience the greater glory that God desires for us.

# THE SEDUCTION OF INFLUENCE

Over the last ten years of my life, since engaging in heavy schedules of traveling and ministering, I have walked into indescribable, incredible experiences.

Staring into video cameras that broadcast what I prophesy around the world, standing on national stages under the spotlight with all eyes on me, preaching from the platforms of mega churches and seeing the sea of people desperate for a word from God, being promised crazy amounts of money and more open doors if I do this or say that—the pressures, applause, temptations, offers, seductions, compromise, identity crises, and insecurities cannot be understood by those who have not experienced them.

Most of us picture ourselves speaking the truth without compromise if given these opportunities, as I have discovered from talking with the many Christians I have encountered over this period. The truth is that no one knows what really motivates them until they actually stand on huge stages and national platforms, are offered huge amounts of money and open doors, and must resist the constant pressures and deceptions of compromise. I have made some of the hardest choices of my life over the last ten years, and they are not one-time choices but choices I know I must face again every time I accept an invitation to speak or step onto a platform. To refuse to be bought with fame, money, and applause when these things are constantly shoved in your face is incredibly difficult.

Around every corner of promotion and new opportunity is a viper waiting to strike, a python waiting to squeeze, a Jezebel looking to silence you, a Saul throwing a javelin, a traitor ready to assassinate your success, and, perhaps most dangerous of all, people lining up to worship you!

As someone who has walked this path and only escaped by the grace of God—knowing the tests will only increase in quantity and difficulty in the years ahead—can I beseech the Church to intercede for those being promoted and given national favor and influence? While it may appear that such leaders "have it all," the truth is that the devil is looking for a hole in their armor and when he finds it, he will penetrate it.

Without our fervent cries for protection and purity for them, another generation of messengers will become prideful, arrogant, compromised, and polluted.

If those called by God only understood the seduction and temptations in ministry, they would stop craving platforms and microphones. The very spotlight many can't wait to step into is the very spotlight that will expose them and turn them into another evangelistic, apostolic, and prophetic whore.

I know this is strong language, but it is serious business in the kingdom of God. It's one thing to not care about a platform because you have never been given one; it's another to walk in great influence, yet refuse to be pimped and prostituted.

Church history is full of men and women who had been tested by obscurity but failed the test of notoriety miserably. The worst thing that can befall a man or woman called by God is to be promoted before he or she is ready. To those of you hungry for influence, lured by the trap of self-promotion into seeking national stages and conferences, please think twice about what doors you are trying to knock down and for what you are asking!

Influence is dangerous. It will eat you alive and make you its mistress. It will steal your time and those gifts that are among the most precious that God gives— your real friends and your family.

Ministry addicts manage all their success at the expense of spending intimate time with God. They expand their ministry and shrink their hearts. The constant phone calls, emails, and text messages will feed ego and create a false identity. Ministry addicts become entitled; they demand honorariums and special treatment. He or she becomes so full of self, there is less and less room for God.

Prophets and intercessors weep over such ones and try to warn them, but ministry addicts won't listen because they have put themselves beyond the need for correction and personal repentance. Oh, emerging generation of voices with growing influence, I fear for you because I know the journey ahead! I know you will not realize your tendency to prioritize people before ministry to God without the fervent prayers of intercessors and the presence of fathers who will rebuke you and speak truth to you.

The truth must be told, regardless of how badly it offends us.

## A PRAYER FOR THE CHURCH

*Father, have Your way in this nation and in the nations of the earth. I am overcome with an intense burden and great weeping. We must have ministers full of purity, integrity, and the fresh anointing. We must have preachers, worship leaders, and saints who value ministering to You more than they value ministering to people. God, break the back of ministry addiction in the Church and let the sons of Zadok arise! Let us recognize that Your judgment is upon Your house in a far greater capacity than we wish to admit.*

## Chapter Four

# A FRESH CALL TO INTIMACY

*W*e are moving into a time and season in the Church when great authority is going to be released over disease, demons, regions, and territories, but the *authority* God is going to release can only be granted and accessed through fresh *intimacy* with Him. God recently said to me, "Jeremiah, large portions of the Church are crumbling because leaders continue to be given keys of authority who have quit on intimacy." In other words, leadership positions should never be given based solely off of gifting but rather granted through faithfulness in the secret place.

The issue here is a serious one. Leaders are hindered from admitting their lack of intimacy with God because the saints require a higher level of consecration in their leaders than they do of themselves. Consequently, leaders (including myself) buckle under the pressure of the saints' need for them to appear super spiritual; leaders are expected to make up in their own walks what is missing in their followers' walks.

While leading a church leadership retreat last year, two main issues surfaced during the three days of our gatherings:

1. There was a fight for holding on to his or her first love (Jesus Christ) in every church

leader's life. Meeting the needs of people was difficult to balance with meeting deep personal needs for time with God.

2. No leader had a safe zone in his or her personal life for sharing real issues about family, marriage, and self. Few leaders had anyone they could trust with their vulnerabilities.

Without divine intervention where we address the need for fresh intimacy in the Church, especially among church leaders, *and* a realm of transparency and vulnerability where there are covenant relationships where heart issues can be shared, the Church and its leaders just go through the motions, let their gifts function (whatever they might be), and we become like the church of Sardis in Revelation 3:1 where Jesus says that while we might have the *appearance* of being alive, but really "you are dead"!

In other words, Jesus is saying to large portions of His Church, "You might be able to fool the people around you and even yourself, but I am the One who judges the thoughts and motivations of your heart."

"I want to warn you," says God, "busyness in the ministry does not equal fruitfulness!"

Years ago, at another gathering of several hundred church leaders, I stood in the pulpit and prophesied to them, "We must not become so busy taking care of the Father's Vineyard (horizontal ministry) that we forget to abide in the Vine (vertical ministry)!"

*All true ministry to God's people must flow from ministry to God.* When church leaders cannot find sufficient time in their schedules to minister to the Lord and break the cycle of ministry addiction, what hope do their followers have?

Are there any sons of Zadok in the land?

## THE MAN OF AUTHORITY

Perhaps the real need is to reexamine the life and ministry of Jesus Christ. He alone is the supreme example for all of us who seek a greater measure of intimacy with God.

In Mark 1:21-22, Mark writes, "They went into Capernaum; and immediately on the Sabbath He entered the synagogue and began to teach. They were amazed at His teaching; for He was teaching them as one having authority, and not as the scribes."

People had heard the teaching of the scribes and Pharisees most of their lives, but when Jesus Christ comes on the scene and starts talking, they notice something on His words. Again, in verse 27 the people exclaim, "What is this? A new teaching with authority!" What was it about the teaching of Jesus that triggered this strong response from the crowd?

The answer is revealed in verse thirty-five when the Word of God says, "In the early morning, while it was still dark, Jesus got up, left the house, and went away to a secluded place, and was praying there." The secret to the authority that Jesus Christ carried and walked in was revealed in His intimacy with the Father. In fact, true spiritual authority is born from intimacy. All activity in the kingdom of God that is not born from intimacy is illegal! Such activity is unauthorized because it was never given permission and seen in the life of Jesus Christ.

## THEY HAD BEEN WITH JESUS

In Acts 4 Peter and John were performing many miraculous signs and wonders among the people. Luke writes in verse thirteen that the religious leaders marveled and began to recognize that Peter and John had been with Jesus. Days are quickly approaching in the Church when there will be such a fresh intimacy and prioritization of vertical ministry to the Lord that many will marvel and be astonished as in the time of

Jesus and Peter and John. Sons of Zadok are arising who carry true spiritual authority because they have spent their lives on their faces at the altar and learning what it means to minister beyond the veil. They will expose the judgment of God upon the Church because of the addiction to horizontal ministry and seek to restore vertical ministry in the sanctuaries of the Lord. There is a cleansing judgment that must come before the true glory and outpouring of the Holy Spirit manifests.

Speaking of the coming judgment on the house of God, R. Loren Sandford boldly claims: "I do not believe that we can merely pray for the cleansing of the prophetic stream [or the Church] and expect it to happen. The culture of self and the prosperity cult that comes with it will not flee shrieking in terror or simply because we want it to or because we prayed a few puny prayers. I believe we must expect, pray, and even long for a cleansing judgment to come. ...The Body of Christ needs its prophetic voices to be holy, pure, and functioning at full strength in order to play the role God wants them to play in this strategic time in the history of the world."[1]

I say—let the cleansing judgment come!

# THE CONVICTION OF THE HOLY SPIRIT

Perhaps you are reading this book and feeling the over-whelming sense of conviction from the Holy Spirit drawing you back to the place of fresh intimacy with Him. As a church leader and traveling minister, I have had to repent again and again for prioritizing people before God. There is an opportunity even today and in this season of your life to make the appropriate shifts and changes to put Jesus Christ back at the center of your life and ministry. We can pray and long together for God to release His cleansing judgment upon His house and our lives. This is a heartfelt prayer that says, "Father, if there is anything in my life that is hindering deep love and affection with You, expose and remove it now."

When it manifests in our lives, God's redemp-tive and cleansing judgment confronts and wipes out anything that stands in the way of love. This is why David prayed in Psalm 139:23-24, "Search me, O God, and know my heart; try me and know my anxious thoughts; and see if there be any hurtful way in me, and lead me in the everlasting way."

God's cleansing judgment is coming upon His Church to prepare them for His Glory. But what of those people who do not belong to His Church?

Is there a destructive judgment that comes to those who are not in Christ?

# NOTE

1. R. Loren Sandford, *Purifying the Prophetic* (Grand Rapids, MI: Chosen Books, 2005), 42.

*Chapter Five*

# NEW COVENANT JUDGMENT

$\mathcal{I}$'m well aware that there are some reading this book in spite of its title.

In fact, I have encountered several Charismatic leaders in the body of Christ who completely deny the existence of any such thing as "new covenant judgment." These leaders believe that since Jesus Christ died on the cross, all judgment has now been suspended until the final judgment seat when He returns (see 2 Cor. 5:10). I could not disagree more with these leaders.

I am convinced that millions of people have been led into a very dangerous place in their assumptions about their faith by this type of hyper-grace theology. Furthermore (particularly after my encounter with the two angels described in Chapter One), I believe the Church will never experience the outpouring or inhabit the realm of glory God is desiring to release until judgment has cleansed His house.

## THE OLD AND NEW TESTAMENT WITNESS

Let me state it plainly.

Jesus did not come to abolish the Old Testament.

A false contrast has been created in parts of the body of Christ that says the Old Testament is the law and the New Testament is grace. The tension between law and grace applies to the means by which we obtain salvation and not to the truth or eternal validity of the revealed Word of God.

God does not change. His will and His character do not change from one testament to the other.

As Hebrews 13:8 says, "Jesus Christ is the same yesterday and today and forever."

Regarding the authority of the Old Testament, Jesus said in Matthew 5:17-18, "Do not think I came to abolish the Law or the Prophets; I did not come to abolish but to fulfill. For truly I say to you, until heaven and earth pass away, not the smallest letter or stroke shall pass from the Law until all is accomplished." The Law accomplished its purpose of demonstrating God's holiness and our guilt, pointing to Jesus as the atonement for our sins. His sacrifice on the Cross set us free from the curse of failure and made grace through faith the way back to Him. He did not, however, throw out the Old Testament as the expressed heart and will of the Father.

In chapter 1, verse 17 of his gospel, John writes, "For the Law was given through Moses; grace and truth came through Jesus Christ." But we know from Scripture that there is grace throughout the Old Testament. It simply came into its fullness through

Jesus. So, grace was neither inaugurated nor instituted with the death and resurrection of Jesus Christ. It was rather "revealed" and "realized" (see the NASB). It existed in the heart of God and His dealings with His people from eternity. Grace expresses who God was, is, and always will be.

Furthermore, Paul, the teacher and affirmer of grace, wrote in Second Timothy 3:16-17 that "All Scripture is inspired by God and profitable for teaching, for reproof, for correction, for training in righteousness; so that the man of God may be adequate, equipped for every good work." By "all scripture," Paul must be referencing the Old Testament; the New Testament had not been written yet. He is clearly affirming the value of the Old Testament in equipping saints for life and ministry.

In this context, we must affirm the validity of the Old Testament and its agreement with the New Testament even as we discuss something apparently as controversial as "New Covenant judgment." To believe and proclaim that the God of the New Testament is not the same God as the God of the Old Testament is a grave doctrinal error with sobering consequences.

In fact, the New Testament identifies three groups of people who are or will experience God's judgment—unbelievers, pretenders to the faith, and believers.

# UNBELIEVERS AND JUDGMENT

John the Baptist's first words to unbelievers urged them to "flee from the coming wrath" (Matt. 3:7 NIV). Paul wrote in Romans 1:18, "For the wrath of God is revealed from heaven against all ungodliness and unrighteousness of men who suppress the truth in unrighteousness." John the Beloved writes in John 3:36 that "He who believes in the Son has eternal life; but he who does not obey the Son will not see life, but the wrath of God abides on him."

John the Baptist's first message to unbelievers exhorted them to flee from *coming* wrath. Paul says that God's wrath is *being revealed*. John declares that God's wrath *abides* upon unbelievers.

Where unbelievers are concerned, the wrath and judgment of God is not only present and future, but in the process of being revealed against them.

There are more New Covenant examples of the wrath and judgment of God upon unbelievers:

- In Acts 12:20–24, King Herod is struck dead by an angel of the Lord for not giving God glory.

- In Acts 13:8–11, Elymas the magician is struck blind by the hand of the Lord for being a fraud and a son of the devil.

- In Revelation 2:22, Jezebel is thrown on a bed of sickness and struck with deadly disease because of her adultery.

## PRETENDERS AND JUDGMENT

What about those who claim to be in Christ but are not? In other words, no fruit exists to confirm their supposed repentance. How does God deal with these people in the New Covenant?

Scripture provides some examples:

- In 1 Corinthians 5:1–13, the immoral brother is judged and handed over to Satan for the destruction of his flesh so that his soul might be saved.

- In 1 Corinthians 11:27–34, supposed believers are judged and become sick, some even die, for not judging themselves before partaking of the Lord's supper.

- In 1 Timothy 1:20, Hymenaus and Alexander were delivered over to Satan for blasphemy.

# JUDGMENT ON BELIEVERS

According to Romans 5:9, all believers who put their faith in Jesus Christ have been spared and saved from the wrath and judgment of God that leads to eternal punishment. However, believers are not spared from the redemptive and cleansing judgment of God that brings discipline and correction (see Rev. 3:19; 1 Cor. 11:29–32). In First Peter 4:17, the Apostle says, "For it is *time* for judgment to begin with the household of God; and if it begins with us first, what will be the outcome for those who do not obey the gospel of God?"

The outcome for those who do not obey the gospel of God is the wrath of God upon them both in the present and the future in a process of ongoing revelation ("being revealed"). How terrifying! But what of this judgment that Peter says "it's time" for in the household of God?

Could the title of this book, *Judgment on the House of God*, bear good news—the coming of something necessary and even desirable for those longing for greater glory and the outpouring of the Holy Spirit?

The definition of the New Testament Greek words for judgment, *krino* (verb) and *krisis* (noun), applies to the concept of judgment in the Hebrew Old Testament as well. Its root means to cut or separate rather than to punish. Concerning Peter's statement that it is "time for judgment to begin in the house of God," the Tyndale New Testament Commentary says, "While God's coming to possess His people is assured, it cannot be realized without preparatory judgment and purification. First Peter 4:17-18 suggests that those who become Christians need current and continual cleansing before they can share in the heavenly glory that is to come" (see vol. 17). God's redemptive judgment upon believers separates the precious from the vile, the pure from the impure, and the holy from the profane. With this understanding, shouldn't believers long for this kind of judgment and receive it as a gift?

God brings judgment on His house for two primary purposes: first, to discipline, cleanse, separate, and purify those who are His; and second, to expose those who are *not* His in spite of their protestations that they are. In Ezekiel 44, judgment came on the House of Israel clearly to discipline, cleanse, separate, and purify. Because of the emphasis on horizontal ministry and ministry addiction in today's Church, God has once again sent His judgment on His house in order that we might turn from the error of our ways, repent, and restore vertical ministry to His house. As a result, we will see the sons of Zadok raised up once again and God's house of prayer will be restored in the earth.

However, a judgment is coming that will expose those who have the outward appearance and show of being believers but are not the sheep of His pastures. This judgment will be destructive in nature and should be feared.

## JUDGMENT IS NEW COVENANT

Those who remove the active judgment of God from the New Testament do so in the spirit of intellectual dishonesty and an anti-Christ agenda fueled by a desire to create and portray a "god" made after our own image. This is not the God of the Scriptures. Perhaps A.W. Pink challenges what's hiding inside the hearts of so many believers who reject "New Covenant judgment" when he says:

> It is sad to find so many professing Christians who appear to regard the wrath of God as something for which they need to make an apology, or at least they wish there was no such thing. While some would not go so far as to openly admit that they consider it a blemish on God's divine character, yet they are far from regarding it with

delight; they like not to think about it, and they rarely hear it mentioned without a secret resentment rising up in their hearts against it. But what do the Scriptures say? As we turn to them, we find that God has made no attempt to conceal the fact of His wrath. He is not ashamed to make it known that vengeance and fury belong to Him. In fact, a study of the concordance will show that there are more references in Scripture to the anger, fury, and wrath of God, than there are His love and tenderness.[1]

# A Story of Cleansing Judgment

Several years ago, I personally knew a minister to whom God had given a power revelation concerning the cleansing judgment that He was bringing to the Levites from Malachi chapter three. Verses 1-4 say:

*"Behold, I am going to send My messenger, and he will clear the way before Me. And the Lord, whom you seek, will suddenly come to His temple; and the messenger of the covenant, in whom you delight, behold, He is coming," says the Lord of hosts. "But who can endure the day of His coming? And who can stand when He appears? For He is like a refiner's fire and*

*like fullers' soap. He will sit as a smelter and purifier of silver, and He will purify the sons of Levi and refine them like gold and silver, so that they may present to the Lord offerings in righteousness. Then the offering of Judah and Jerusalem will be pleasing to the Lord as in the days of old and as in former years."*

As this minister began to preach this revelation to the body of Christ, little did he realize that God would begin that judgment even on his own life and marriage. Despite numerous warnings from trusted voices in his life, within one year of preaching Malachi 3, this minister had fallen into moral compromise himself. With his marriage suffering great difficulties, he had to step down from ministry altogether and go into deeper inner healing and counseling. By God's grace, they came through it all, but nonetheless this minister came under the cleansing judgment of God and almost lost his marriage and family because of it. The primary purpose of God's judgment upon His own household is always purification, not condemnation. To this day, the minister rejoices concerning how God judged his own life, marriage, and ministry. This story and many others like it are coming to the household of God in order that He might cleanse, purify, and prepare us for the greater glory that is coming!

# NOTE

1. Arthur W. Pink, "The Wrath of God," *Studies in the Scriptures*, Vol. 10, No. 4, April, 1931, p. 73.

*Chapter Six*

# THE SPIRIT OF PERVERSION

*A*bout six months after my encounter with the two angels of cleansing and glory, I was speaking at a prophetic conference in Southern California. As I slept in the hotel one night during the meetings, I had an encounter where I began to wrestle a large demonic principality of perversion that was and had been attaching itself to many charismatic leaders in the body of Christ. As I wrestled with it, a well-known prophet who struggled with homosexuality while he was alive appeared in the distance. Around his body and wrapped up to his neck was a large python snake and his eyes were plucked out. Another well-known Charismatic leader appeared before me, and he too had a large python snake wrapped around his body and up to his neck and his eyes were also plucked out.

God immediately spoke to me in the dream and said, "And when you see all these things come to pass, know then that I am releasing cleansing judgment upon My house. For My people have worshiped these men. My people have failed to discern. In that day, when exposure comes, tell My people to not accuse, to not point the finger, but rather to ask themselves, 'How have I contributed to all of this?' For the judgment that shall come upon My house in the days ahead will directly deal with the idol worship of men and ministries that is an abomination before Me."

I woke up from the dream and lay on my hotel floor, weeping.

That morning I went to the prophetic conference I was speaking at in Lancaster, California, and shared a large portion of my dream. The title of my spontaneous and prophetic message was "Confronting Perversion in the House of God."

God spoke two things to me very clearly the night before. The first was that "this will not go away"; the second warned me that "you have not even heard the half of it."

## Exposing Perversion

A recent survey suggests that over fifty percent of church leaders watch pornography at least twice a month. Millions around the world are watching the news as church leaders are exposed for adultery, sex with minors, and other perverse behaviors. The number of pastors divorcing and remarrying because of sexual misconduct is off the charts.

But what is worse than any of these things is the fact that many of the saints don't even care!

## What Is Happening in the Church Today?

Ezekiel 44:23 defines the roles of the priests/leaders as this: "They shall teach My people the difference between the holy and the profane, and cause them to discern between the unclean and the clean."

Many church leaders are failing on a massive scale to teach God's people the difference between what is holy and what is not because they themselves have become compromised!

Where are the conferences and revival services for pastors and leaders that specifically address the vulnerabilities to pornography and perversion they face in their own lives? Perhaps we don't have more freedom from sexual sin in the pews because there is no freedom coming from behind the pulpit!

The anointing of God flows from the top down. I am prophetically warning the saints that when we submit to leadership that is bound in pornography and perversion, no matter how gifted and/or charismatic they are, our own spirits, marriages, and families will become defiled. We become desensitized to evil and impurity, and our own lives, marriages, and families become vulnerable because of the choices of our spiritual leaders.

By God's grace, as a leader in the body of Christ, I have been pornography free for fifteen years and I have never had a staff member in ten years under my care who struggled with pornography and perversion.

Why do I share this?

Because *there is freedom* available in Jesus Christ. Not all church leaders and staff members are engaged in sexual sin!

There must be a place of vulnerability and transparency among pastors and church staff members where wickedness and sin can be confessed and eradicated from their midst. There has to be a higher standard for Christian leadership in this hour. Who really cares about the entertainment and show that goes on at youth night when our youth pastors are addicted to looking at naked women in private? Who really cares how many people fall down and receive their miracle on Sunday when the man of God is secretly sleeping with a woman in the congregation who is not his wife?

By the way, that worship is not "anointed" when the choir director and bass player are married to other people, but their marriages are actually a cover for the homosexual encounters they have with each other during the week.

Simply put, there has never been a greater need for a new breed of leader, leaders who value purity over gifting. We have never needed saints more than now who will distance themselves from the charismatic hype of a leader as they evaluate that leader's marriage and children from a biblical standpoint.

Want to go to a revival service or conference? Don't be impressed with the charisma of gifting of the leader. Do some research and find out whether their marriage and/or family is a wreck or not. Hear the word of the Lord in this hour concerning the pornography and perversion among church leadership:

> *"Both prophet and priest are godless; even in my temple I find their wickedness...Woe to the shepherds who are destroying and scattering the sheep of my pasture! ...I myself will gather the remnant of my flock...I will place shepherds over them who will tend them, and they will no longer be afraid or terrified, nor will any be missing," declares the Lord* (Jeremiah 23:11; 23:1,3-4 NIV).

## WHEN SIN BECOMES TRIVIAL

The author of First Kings 16:30-31 records that "Ahab the son of Omri did evil in the sight of the Lord more than all who were before him. It came about, as though it had been a trivial thing for him to walk in the sins of Jeroboam the son of Nebat, that he married Jezebel the daughter of Ethbaal king of the Sidonians, and went to serve Baal and worshiped him."

*Trivial* is defined as "of little value or importance." King Ahab was more wicked than all those who came before him because his approach to sin was careless and casual. What he failed to recognize was that a causal approach to sin produces casualties.

Notice the connection between his attitude toward sin and his marriage with Jezebel, one of the most seductive and evil women of all time. When we do not take sin seriously in our lives, it opens the door to the spirit of perversion. We begin to crave and become attracted to things and people we would otherwise never find attractive. Because Ahab considered sin a trivial matter, it produced unrighteous affections in his heart, opening a demonic gateway for Jezebel to enter, rule, and ruin his life.

## Covenant Over Compromise

According to verse 34 in First Kings 16, during Ahab's reign, the city of Jericho and its gates were rebuilt and the cost of rebuilding the city was Hiel the Bethelite's first and youngest sons. Damon Thompson asks the question, "What kind of man would intentionally do something that would cost him his own sons?"

The answer is a perverted man!

Damon Thompson again comments on this verse, pointing out that "One generation's compromise becomes another generation's captivity."

Could pornography be the great Goliath of this generation? When fathers watch pornography, it costs them their own families because they pass that stronghold to their children. When fathers fail to realize that watching pornography is fellowshipping with demons, they sacrifice their sons and daughters to those demonic powers.

In a generation in which many church leaders and saints have compromised with perversion and pornography, God is raising up covenant men and women to reverse the curse. No matter how perverse a church culture may become, a covenant man or woman can make the place of cursing become the place of promise. If there is perversion in our lives, somewhere in our past we have adopted the attitude that sin is a trivial thing.

## True Repentance from Sin

A.T. Robertson, one of the greatest Greek scholars of his day, stated that the New Testament position on repentance could be summed up in the following words: "Change your mind *and life*. Turn right about and do it *now*." According to the *New International Dictionary of New Testament Theology*, "The predominantly intellectual understanding of 'metanoia' as a change of mind plays very little part in the NT. Rather the decision by the whole man to completely turn his life around is stressed over and over again."

Saints, true repentance is far more than a "changing of your mind" or an "adjustment of your thinking" as hyper-grace preachers declare. Repentance is a lifestyle change. Strongholds of sin are demolished, hardened hearts break open, and the grip of Satan is loosed by the power of the blood of Jesus Christ.

Biblical repentance means: *Turn around! Turn back to God! Turn away from your sins and turn to Him! Make an about-face!* The proof of genuine repentance is found in our actions, not our confessions.

## PLUMB LINE PREACHERS

Watch for the emergence of plumb line preachers in the earth carrying a specific mandate to confront and remove the spot and wrinkle from the Bride prior to the return of the Bridegroom. These covenant men and women of God will be like hot irons plucked from the fire. They will press in and apply great pressure to anything and everything that is unclean and defiled.

They will be oracles of righteousness, messengers gripped by repentance and the fear of the Lord, prophets who despise and weep over wickedness and sin. They are forerunners, deliverers, and faithful to the truth no matter what it costs them. Their convictions are fierce, their consecration is intense, and everyone just wants them to tone it down and stop crying out. These plumb line preachers are Nazarites—pure ones—separated unto God through long seasons of prayer and fasting. They sing one octave too high for the religious church.

These righteous ones are called to prepare the Bride for her Bridegroom. They have been branded with the need for a "pure and spotless" Bride.

*Chapter Seven*

ADDRESSING THE SINS OF ELI

*I*n First Samuel 3:1, we encounter a young boy named Samuel ministering to the Lord under the old priest Eli. In a day when the word of the Lord was rare, God raised up a young prophet who would restore the priestly function to the prophetic ministry of his day.

May it be so now among the nations of the earth!

Surrounding Samuel was a compromised priesthood embodied in Eli and his two sons, Hophni and Phinehas. Eli as a father failed to confront the sins of his sons. When their sinfulness grew so rank it required his intervention, he was too late to do them any good, for "they would not listen to the voice of their father, for the Lord desired to put them to death" (1 Sam. 2:25).

One of the primary roles of fathers in the house of God is to establish a clear standard of morality that sons and daughters can follow. When young people choose to compromise, they should be able to find fathers of covenant who can lovingly discipline, correct, and teach them the ways of the Lord. It was not so in the days of Eli, and in many places today it is not so in the house of God.

In fact, I fear that a spirit of Eli has come upon far too many church leaders in this hour, who are breeding a generation of Hophnis and Phinehases in the Church because of it. In an attempt to be relevant, too many Christian leaders, baby boomers in their '50s, '60s, and '70s, are betraying their followers' trust by refusing to address sin in the Church. As a result, a generation of twenty-, thirty-, and forty-year-olds have little or no fear of the Lord and continue to engage in gross immortality and darkness while believing the lie that they are somehow born again and even fit for ministry.

In the midst of rampant perversion and a refusal to take a stand, I see God raising up an army of intercessors who understand this revelation (an army of Hannahs) and they will begin to birth and mother the rise of pure "Samuel prophets" in our day. These Samuels will call out church leaders operating in a spirit of Eli and demand repentance from the generation of Hophnis and Phinehases in the Church.

## SANCTIFIED YOUTH INTERCOURSE

A growing number of young adults, eighteen- to thirty-five-year-olds I meet across the USA as I travel and minister, believe and are being encouraged by older people to solve their "burning with lust" problem by getting married. In other words, they are encouraged to have "sanctified intercourse" apart from the

sanctified motives and pure desires that real relationship creates between two people.

Let me be clear, Christian young people! If your
primary reason for getting married is for sex or because
you can't wait or you couldn't wait and are already
messed up, you are probably not in love. On the con-
trary, you probably have self-control issues that need
to be addressed before you consider marriage. Getting
in bed with someone does not deliver us from an
addiction to pornography or the destructive insecurities that cause us to throw hearts and bodies at anyone
who takes notice of us. In fact, self-control is essential
to marital success.

We need more Christian young people who will
invest themselves in *long* engagements where intercourse is not an option and focused time is given to
knowing one another in spirit and in truth! This is real
love! This is the means to end the *terrible* divorce rates
in the Church.

Pastors, please stop marrying young people just
because they have already had sex or can't wait. Is
sex the purpose of marriage? Really?! A sexual revo-
lution is coming to Christian young people, and it is
this: Make righteous choices, get delivered from lust
and pornography, have a long engagement with *no*

*intercourse*, receive solid premarital counseling. Then enjoy an incredible marriage!

## PROPHETIC PROSTITUTION EXPOSED

I see a trend rising in the house of God where prophets are acting like and being treated as magicians, prostitutes, and pimps. On stages and throughout the internet, many offer their prophetic services to anyone who can fill their pockets with money, promote their ministry, and fuel book sales.

These men and women are acting like modern-day prophetic whores. They are stimulated by stroking the egos and flesh of leaders and people alike, all at the expense of ignoring the purity and fresh anointing we so desperately need in the prophetic movement.

Like Eli's sons Hophni and Phinehas in First Samuel 2, these unsanctified messengers are engaging in wickedness and sin in the house of God because they treat that which is holy and pure as casual and a joke. The spirit of mammon has devoured these "prophets for hire." They have been ravaged by a greed for financial gain and a lust to be treated with all the perks and accommodations that a Hollywood actor would be given.

Just as Jeremiah declared in Jeremiah 23:13, many prophets in the earth are "prophesying by Baal" and leading the body of Christ astray. The Baal spirit has caused the prophets' focus and concern to be on personal gain when they should be agonizing over the sins of a nation and travailing over how to bring forth messages of repentance, reformation, and revival. People are being stroked to sleep when God desires to provoke His people to change.

Some high-profile contemporary prophets now require people to scan their credit cards or sow large seed offerings in order to receive a word from God. How the Holy Spirit grieves when people line up by the droves to pay these prophetic prostitutes for their illicit spiritual "favors"!

Prophets cannot minister in this kind of atmosphere without partnering with the spirit of witchcraft. Many church leaders who have themselves lost the fresh anointing of the Holy Spirit and lead failing ministries are inviting prophetic voices into their ministries in an attempt to gather large offerings and bolster their declining attendance. These pastors are Sauls looking for Samuels to prop them up. Such prophets and leaders have made a demonic covenant with mammon and witchcraft before their prophetic meetings begin. Such sick and twisted practices must not scam the people of God. He is nowhere to be found in the midst of this evil idolatry!

God is not going to shut down the prophetic movement, but He is about to clean it up! There is a holy confrontation about to take place between the true prophets of God and the unholy ones. The contamination and pollution that has infiltrated the house of God must be exposed and repented of in order for the angel of glory to come.

## FATHERS AND ICHABOD

When fathers no longer confront sin in the house of God, His glory will depart from their midst even though many are not aware of the departure. If the saints are attending a church or ministry where sin is not being confronted on a regular basis and calls for repentance are not being issued, they are in danger of fellowshipping in a house where God is not honored. God is not pleased.

A good-looking young adult couple recently approached me at an altar asking for a prophetic word of blessing regarding their relationship. Expecting me to quickly bless them in response to their request, they bowed their heads.

I did not have to seek the Lord for my question.

"Are you two sleeping together?" I asked.

The look on their faces as their heads snapped up was priceless. There was no need for an answer.

"You are asking me to bless something that the Word of God has clearly already called sinful," I said. "You don't need a prophetic word. What you need to do is repent of your sins, stop sleeping together, separate, and then I'll pray God's blessings upon you."

The couple marched from that church faster than I could blink and gave me the middle finger on their way out the door.

To be completely transparent, as I continue to preach all over the USA and world, I am fully convinced that if the uncompromised gospel of Jesus Christ was boldly preached with authority in our churches, many of them would empty rather than fill. Sexual immorality is at the top of almost every list of sins in the New Testament, and it is emphasized in the book of Revelation as one of Satan's primary weapons against the Church in the end times (see Rev. 2:20; 9:21; 14:8; 17:1-4).

Lifting our hands up on Sunday morning and being promiscuous on Friday night is not okay. Heterosexual, homosexual, bisexual, and however else sexual you want to get, if it is not in covenant as defined by the Word (man and woman) then God condemns it. Saints, the sin of sexual immorality is not just in the pews! Unfortunately, it's behind some of the pulpits and strutting on stage behind the keyboard and in the choir.

I believe God is releasing bold prophetic messengers in this hour who will specifically confront the sin of sexual immorality in the Church and raise up a standard of righteousness in the land. Now is the time to drop the plumb line, make true disciples, and fulfill the great commission. Preach the Word in love and stop apologizing for it!

## THE SPEAR OF PHINEHAS

On Yom Kippur I dreamed about the spear of Phinehas. Numbers 25 details the story of Israel as they camped at a place called Shittim in an area occupied by the Moabites. The Moabites were an idolatrous, sinful people who prided themselves in all manner of sexual sins that they committed continuously. While camped there, a large group of Israelites decided to deliberately rebel against God by "play[ing] the harlot with the daughters of Moab" (Num. 25:1).

These strange women subsequently enticed many Israelite men through sexual perversion to commit the sin of idolatry and worship demonic false gods. According to Numbers, the anger of God broke out against Israel and a plague afflicted them. God commanded Moses to instruct the chief of each tribe to put to death each member of his tribe who committed the sin of idolatry.

Suddenly, "An Israelite man brought into the camp a Midianite woman right before the eyes of Moses and the whole assembly of Israel while they were weeping at the entrance to the tent of meeting. When Phinehas son of Eleazar, the son of Aaron, the priest, saw this, he left the assembly, took a spear in his hand and followed the Israelite into the tent. He drove the spear into both of them, right through the Israelite man and into the woman's stomach. Then the plague against the Israelites was stopped" (Num. 25:6-7 NIV).

God spoke through Moses and said, "Phinehas son of Eleazar, the son of Aaron, the priest, has turned my anger away from the Israelites. Since he was as zealous for my honor among them as I am, I did not put an end to them in my zeal. Therefore tell him I am making my covenant of peace with him. He and his descendants will have a covenant of a lasting priesthood, because he was zealous for the honor of his God and made atonement for the Israelites" (Num. 25:10-13 NIV).

In the prophetic dream on Yom Kippur, I saw God handing out "spears of Phinehas" to specific individuals in the earth who had consecrated themselves and taken a strong stand for righteousness and holiness in the midst of a church culture of compromise. I specifically saw him hand a spear to Todd White. "Phinehas" means a "jaw of brass." We are entering into an era in the body of Christ when mouthpieces of truth and messengers with foreheads like Ezekiel will arise (see Ezek. 3:9).

In Numbers 25, Phinehas made atonement for the sins of the people and the plague ceased because he rose up in the jealousy and zeal of God. Because of this, God made a special covenant with Phinehas, a covenant of jealousy, that a perpetual priesthood would be his forever. In other words, his actions purchased grace for his family line for generations to come.

Yom Kippur is a day for remembering and celebrating the all-sufficient sacrifice of Jesus Christ on the cross, that Christ truly has made atonement for our sins. But we should also prophetically recognize on this day and in this year that God is releasing spears of Phinehas to uncompromised voices of truth that will actually hold back the plagues that are coming to the body of Christ because of the rampant sexual immorality and sin. God is searching the earth seeking to strengthen and stir up those who are willing to cry aloud and spare not.

God is a jealous God who is inviting us into a realm of holiness and separation from the things of the world like never before. He is preparing His Bride to be without spot and wrinkle upon His return. Now is the time to rise up and take a stand for righteousness in our lives, families, and churches. Now is the time to drop the plumb line.

## RESTORING FALLEN CHURCH LEADERS

When a leader in the body of Christ has fallen into sin, whether sexual immorality, drunkenness, financial misappropriation, or other in kind, the Bible provides a clear path to address these issues. Here are the three steps in order:

1. Repentance—not just sorrow but true repentance going back to the root.

2. Reconciliation—cleaning up the mess, making things right with those who have been affected.

3. Restoration—the leader is to be restored back to God; second, he or she is to be restored back to spouse and family; third, he or she is to be restored back to the body of Christ; and finally, he or she is possibly

to be restored back to ministry, but this is not mandatory.

Unfortunately, in many Christian circles the central focus of restoration for fallen church leaders has centered on the restoration to ministry, whether it be to preaching, miracles, the prophetic, pastoring, teaching, or the exercise of some other gifting or ministry. The truth is that if the only reason church leaders who have fallen are willing to repent is so that they can get "back into ministry," they are have not really repented. Quite frankly, such people are addicted to ministry, and people who are addicted to ministry do not need to be serving in ministry.

The quickness with which we restore fallen church leaders is often a sign that we value them for their giftings rather than for their holiness. We should pray for all the families and spouses of leaders in the body of Christ who have fallen. May God surround each and every one of us with men and women of wise counsel who will love us enough to speak the truth.

# Chapter Eight

## RIGHTEOUS MOTHERS ARISE!

*As* God showed me the spirit of Eli resting upon many fathers in large portions of the Church who refuse to confront the wickedness and sin of the next generation, my soul was vexed with deep grief. After much travail and intercession, God began to speak to me concerning the days of Deborah, who is called a "mother in Israel" (see Judg. 5).

In Judges, Deborah, the only female judge, summons Barak, a male, to lead the army of Israel into battle. Barak refuses to go unless Deborah comes with him. Her response is straightforward and simple: "The honor will not be yours, for the Lord will deliver Sisera into the hands of a woman" (Judg. 4:9 NIV).

The Church is moving into an era in which righteous mothers are going to arise and inherit the mandate that God has given fathers. Note the details in the biblical description of her: "She used to sit under the palm tree of Deborah...and the sons of Israel came up to her for judgment" (Judg. 4:5). The palm tree speaks of Deborah's humility and secret life in God. God raised Deborah to judge and lead a nation because of the absence of pride and arrogance in her. Deborah's strength lay in her freedom from any need to be seen or heard.

# A Vision of Righteous Mothers

In a prophetic vision, I saw these Deborahs taking their place in the body of Christ globally. They will walk in such a purity, humility, and standard of righteousness that great conviction of sin will come upon sons and daughters. The days of "wait until your father gets home" are ending and the days of "your mother already knows what you are doing" are here. These days are not going away. Discerning mothers will cut off the plans of the enemy before they have opportunity to manifest. Righteous mothers leading sons and daughters in the paths of Yahweh will be one of the greatest hidden blessings in this generation.

# The Power of Praying Mothers

Hannah, who was barren, longed to have children but God had closed her womb. She entered the temple and the Scriptures say, "Now Eli the priest was sitting on the seat by the doorpost of the temple of the Lord" (1 Sam. 1:9). Again, take careful notice that Eli (a father) was called to stand before the Lord, not sit. This was a prophetic signal that the priesthood had already become compromised. Eli could no longer stand before Yahweh because he had lost the anointing and zeal for the house of God. While a father refused to stand for a generation, God was preparing Hannah, a praying mother, to give birth to a new generation of pure prophets who would restore God's divine order in the land.

## MOTHER INTERCESSORS

A generation of intercessory women will become burdened like never before for the restoration of the purity and fear of the Lord in the house of God. The travail of childbirth for the spiritual health of the next generation will overtake them. Many of these women will never have a place of high visibility in the Church, but their prayers will shake the gates of hell and bust heaven open for the sons and daughters. Through fasting and prayer, they will break the power of addiction and call many prodigals back home. It will be glorious!

## THE KISS OF BROKENNESS

One of the primary callings of the righteous mothers who are arising is to minister to the brokenness of this next generation and teach them the true power of the secret place. I recently received a prophetic dream where I went to a large stadium full of youth and young adults. They were gathered there seeking direction, affirmation, and encouragement from the Father.

As I watched them cry out to God, I saw lips from heaven come down and kiss the masses. Liquid honey drenched the entire crowd gathered there.

God immediately spoke to me in the dream and said, "I am kissing My Bride with brokenness in this hour. This is a most precious gift that I am giving her. Religion has taught the people to hide and mask brokenness, but where My Spirit is allowed to move freely, brokenness is embraced and welcomed. Brokenness is the alabaster box that I am worthy of and I am asking this next generation to come now and lay down at My feet. I see many pretty alabaster boxes, but not many that have allowed me to break them."

As the liquid honey began to drench the entire crowd gathered there, many in the stadium were visibly upset and began washing the honey off of themselves very quickly. I asked the Holy Spirit what was happening as I felt immense grief come over me in the dream. He said to me, "So many in this generation are seeking promotion and influence that they do not understand that the place of divine validation is in the wilderness, not on a platform. They are ready to stand up and preach, when I am calling them to learn how to pray and lead from their knees. Beware of the voices in this generation that will stroke the carnality of man by promising fame, riches, and greatness. Watch for those who will call this generation to the secret place where I will mantle them with a spirit of brokenness and humility like never before. The higher the calling and grace, the deeper the crushing will be. To those who refuse the kiss of brokenness, they will walk with human ambition and call it *vision from above,* and they will run and prophesy when I have not spoken to them."

Upon waking up from this prophetic dream, prayer made it clear to me that God was highlighting two specific groups. First are those who would quickly wash the honey off of themselves and reject God's kiss of brokenness. The Spirit said in the dream, "To those who refuse the kiss of brokenness, they will walk with human ambition and call it *vision from above,* and they will run and prophesy when I have not spoken to them." He also said, "So many in this generation are seeking promotion and influence when I am calling them to the wilderness. Beware of the voices who are promising fame, riches, and greatness."

As God kisses this generation with brokenness, desiring to address issues of pride, selfish ambition, and a love for platforms and microphones, voices will arise that will encourage them in this deception instead. They will promise popularity and greatness and lead many astray. We must allow God to expose the intentions and attitudes of the many hearts pursuing "ministry" when they should be pursuing devotion to Jesus more than anything else.

The second group in the dream brings great joy to my heart! God is raising up broken mothers right now who will lead this young generation into the wilderness and establish their identity as the Beloved apart from all ministry! God is going to mantle these sons and daughters with a spirit of humility and brokenness like never before. Look for weeping messengers who carry a special anointing for tears and brokenness to be released upon this generation.

Young generation, will we allow the Father to kiss us with brokenness in the secret place or will we continue to idolize platforms and popularity and fall into great deception? May the righteous mothers arise in this hour to help mentor, disciple, and lead this next generation through their deep brokenness. And out of the sons' and daughters' immense pain, I believe a mighty prophetic company of true voices being watched over by intercessory mothers is going to shift the global landscape of the Church. Even so, let it be, Lord!

*Chapter Nine*

# THE SPIRIT AND POWER OF ELIJAH

As God continues to address the spirit of Eli resting on many spiritual fathers in the Church and raises up righteous mothers in the land, what about the fathers who have been faithful to declare the word of the Lord over many years? Will God hold the sons and daughters responsible who have refused to listen to these noble fathers? Malachi declared that God would, "send you Elijah the prophet before the coming of the great and terrible day of the Lord. He will restore the hearts of the fathers to their children and the hearts of the children to their fathers, so that I will not come and smite the land with a curse" (Mal. 4:5-6). In the last days, the days that we now live in, the Scriptures say we are going to witness a tremendous reconciliation between fathers and sons.

Recently I felt very stirred to reexamine what several faithful spiritual fathers spoke in their dying days to the generation they lived in. We live in a day and age when many are crying out, "Where are the spiritual fathers?" Perhaps an equally valid cry should be rising in the land: "Where are the sons and daughters?"

The hearts of the fathers are to be restored to the sons and daughters, but the hearts of the sons and daughters must also be restored to the fathers! In Exodus 20:12, God charges us to "honor your father and your mother, that your days may be prolonged in the land which the Lord your God gives you."

Jesus exhorts us to "Honor [our] father and mother," warning that "he who speaks evil of father or mother is to be put to death" (Matt. 15:4).

I believe God is saying that we have not heeded, honored, or stewarded the voices of our spiritual fathers in this generation. Is there a curse on the Church for failing to honor our spiritual fathers?

Many great generals and fathers of the faith have gone to be with the Lord over the last twenty-five years. Bill Bright (the founder and director of Campus Crusade for Christ), Oral Roberts, David Wilkerson, Leonard Ravenhill, and Billy Graham are but a few of the most prominent.

What have these spiritual fathers said to us? Who knows what they said in their dying days?

# THE VOICES OF THE FATHERS

In 1995, in his book *The Coming Revival*, Bill Bright called two million Americans to forty days of fasting and prayer, asking God to have mercy on America and not send Judgment on her. "God does not tolerate sin," wrote Bright, "The Bible and history make this painfully clear." He continued:

I believe God has given ancient Israel as an example of what will happen to the United States without revival. He will continue to discipline us with all kinds of problems until we repent or until we are destroyed, as was ancient Israel because of her sins and disobedience.[1]

In 1999, David Wilkerson authored a book called *America's Last Call*. His words echo those of Bright:

Our nation right now is receiving its final call to repentance just prior to a great Judgment. Without a return of the church to true repentance, fasting, and prayer, I believe an economic and social collapse is coming, not because I have a prophetic word. Rather, I've simply just studied God's Word and I've discerned from the Scriptures that God is dealing with America in the same way He has dealt with other nations who have forsaken Him. The fact is God's ways are absolutely unchangeable when it comes to His dealings with sinful nations. God works the same in every generation because He is just! (Note the example of Nineveh).[2]

"The righteous man perishes, and no man takes it to heart," mourns Isaiah in chapter 57, verse one. "Devout men are taken away, while no one understands."

Isaiah is telling his readers, "Take note! Do you recognize the critical and transitional hour you are living in? Great men and women die and no one says, 'Where's the next?' No one asks, 'Why?'"

When Moses died, Joshua took over. Are there Joshuas to take over, or will the fathers die and the Word of the Lord become rare? Will we fail to walk in the ways of our fathers as the kings of Israel did?

The propensity of humanity is to reject and ignore the wisdom of the fathers. Eighteen of Israel's kings failed to walk in the ways of their fathers. Eighteen kings ruled in Judah and only half of them walked in the ways of their fathers. In short, three out of every four kings in Israel and Judah did not walk in the ways of their fathers!

Alarming as it is, this statistic aligns with that provided by the parable of the sower—only one fourth of the seed was fit to bring forth fruit.

With this sobering revelation in mind, I turned to the generals and fathers of our day to read and consider their words.

# THE SOUND OF A TRUMPET

In July of 2012, Billy Graham wrote a letter to the Church entitled "My Heart Aches for America." In it, Graham said:

> Some years ago, my wife, Ruth, was reading the draft of a book I was writing. When she finished a section describing the terrible downward spiral of our nation's moral standards and the idolatry of worshiping false gods such as technology and sex, she startled me by exclaiming, "If God doesn't punish America, He'll have to apologize to Sodom and Gomorrah." ...Millions of babies have been aborted and our nation seems largely unconcerned. Self-centered indulgence, pride, and a lack of shame over sin are now emblems of the American lifestyle. ...Our society strives to avoid any possibility of offending anyone—except God. ...My heart aches for America and its deceived people.[3]

In his book *The Emergent Generation*, Thomas Rainer noted that, of those born after 1984, only four percent were actively involved in regular church activity.[4] America has the fifth largest population of young people under eighteen; that is the fifth largest harvest in the world! Out of seventy-five million young people, twenty-four plus million do not live with their biological fathers. Daughters are being raised to marry porn-addicted men who have not been fathered.

After hearing of the judgment coming to his nature, the prophet Jeremiah wept, "O my soul, my soul! I am pained in my very heart! My heart makes a noise in me; I cannot hold my peace, because you have heard, O my soul, the sound of the trumpet, the alarm of war" (Jer. 4:19 NKJV).

## The Nature of an Alarm

When I travel, I often ask, "How many of you have children who have walked away from the Lord?"

Then I ask, "How many prayer meetings are you having for families this week?"

And yet we prance around, saying, "God's in a good mood."

On the first of May in 2014, Ann Graham Lotz, Billy Graham's daughter, stood before those gathered for the National Day of Prayer breakfast and read from the book of Joel (verse 15 NKJV): "Alas, for the day of the Lord is at hand!"

"Do we not see the signs all around us?" she challenged her audience.

## Rude Awakening or Great Awakening

In Matthew 11, Jesus spoke to a generation who were unwilling to hear the Word of the Lord. He characterizes them as a people who want to call the plays, who say to God's messengers: "We played the flute for you, and you did not dance; we sang a dirge, and you did not mourn" (Matt. 11:17).

They did not realize that God sent messengers of kindness (Isaiah, for example, plays the flute in Isaiah 60) to lure them into revival. When God's messengers play the flute, the dance should be revival.

When they play the dirge, the dance should be repentance.

The greatest messenger sent to them—the greatest man born of a woman (see Matt. 11:11)—was John the Baptist, who played the dirge and preached repentance, but they would not dance to God's tune.

Have we listened to our fathers?

## Standing between Two Crises

Joel warns Israel of two impending Judgments: economic collapse (triggered by a locust plague that destroyed crops and food sources) and military crisis. In Joel 1:14-15, he calls the people to a sacred assembly.

Note the very first thing Joel does. He shouts, "Hear! Listen! Before you start figuring out how you are going to pull yourself out of this mess, push 'Pause'! Have you ever seen anything like this in your day?"

In other words, Joel warns his listeners that:

- They had better interpret these events correctly;
- They had better hear correctly;
- They had better respond to the call to prayer!

If we don't hear Joel in his day, we will never hear Jeremiah in his day: "It's not going to be that there is no food," Jeremiah tells his people. "It's going to be that women will be eating their own babies because of the siege of Nebuchadnezzar!"

Joel tells us, "The most important thing you can do right now is *hear!*"

"Announce a fast! Call a solemn assembly! Gather the elders and all the inhabitants of the land into the house of the Lord your God and cry out!"

"Humble yourselves! Pray and seek My face and turn from your wicked ways!" declares God in Second Chronicles 7:14.

*We must hear the voice of our spiritual fathers rightly and communicate it to our children, lest further things come and our children have no ear to hear the prophetic voice!*

If we don't hear in Joel's day, the children in Jeremiah's day will think he's just another bitter prophet.

Joel informs us that the pathway back to God in national crisis is prayer, humility, and fasting.

## THE SPIRIT AND POWER OF ELIJAH IS COMING UPON THIS GENERATION

How do we respond to the voices of the fathers?

First, we must recognize we are in a season of crisis. Are we hearing correctly? Turn off the noise; stop becoming desensitized by evil. It's time to rip our clothes!

Did we just hear what the fathers said?

"Has anything ever happened like this in our day?"

Second, we must discern; we must interpret correctly. We need to exercise the gift of interpretation! Failure to accurately interpret the signs of the times leads to a culture of prayerlessness. We love to ease our consciences and bolster our comfort with wrong biblical principles in an hour of crisis. Biblical counsel differs based on the historical context of a situation.

We witness this in Isaiah 36 and 37. Hezekiah has turned to the Lord and supported His priests. Assyria invades Judah and threatens military conquest, and Isaiah prophesies deliverance from Sennacherib.

Later, in chapter 39, Hezekiah is visited by an official delegation from Babylon celebrating Hezekiah's recovery of health, and Isaiah prophesies destruction.

Later, in Jeremiah, Babylon is the invader. False prophets start prophesying the wrong chapter and verse. "Deliverance is coming," they say.

Jeremiah correctly interprets the time. "No deliverance!" he declares.

We must not confuse our individual standing before God with the corporate status of a nation if we are to walk in the spirit and power of Elijah. The sons and daughters must hear the voices of their spiritual fathers and walk in their ways!

# THE SPIRIT AND POWER OF ELIJAH PRAYER

*For the failure to honor many of the spiritual fathers who have given us the word of the Lord again and again, we repent as sons and daughters for failing to heed their words. If we be under the judgment of God for ignoring what these righteous men declared in their dying days, God, we say that we are sorry. Please lift off the curse from our land and restore honor in Your house once again. Turn the hearts of the sons and daughters back to the fathers, we pray, in the name of Jesus Christ.*

## NOTES

1. Bill Bright, *The Coming Revival.*
2. David Wilkerson, *America's Last Call.*
3. Billy Graham, "My Heart Aches for America," Billy Graham Evangelistic Association, July 19, 2012, https://billygraham.org/story/billy-graham-my -heart-aches-for-america.
4. Thomas Rainer, *The Emergent Generation.*

*Chapter Ten*

# POWER IN THE BLOOD

*I*n the midst of God cleansing and purifying His Church from the spirit of perversion and false grace teaching that excuses sinful behaviors, let us boldly declare that there is power in the blood of Jesus Christ to defeat every stronghold of sin in our lives! I believe a generation of churchgoers has now found itself in deep bondage to sin due in large part to our lack of knowledge and in-depth study of the Word of God. Romans 6 provides an excellent road map for all those seeking greater keys to walking in the true freedom that the grace of God provides for us. Legalists who did not understand the concept of grace posed two questions to Paul in Romans 6. Paul takes his time answering these. *His desire is to show the listeners that true grace is the victorious life over sin.*

## Taking a Step Back

Before we look deeper into Romans 6, however, I want to back up to a statement Paul makes in Romans 5:20 where he says, "but where sin increased, grace abounded all the more." In verse 21 he concludes, "that, as sin reigned in death, even so grace would reign through righteousness to eternal life through Jesus Christ our Lord."

After reading verse twenty of chapter five, one might ask the question, "Paul, do you mean to tell me that God is willing to forgive a person's sins as often as he commits them?" Paul's reply? "Yes!" "Well, then," responds you or I, "if that's the case, shall we Christians keep on habitually sinning in order that God may have an opportunity to forgive us and thus display His grace?"

This is the background of Paul's resounding *"May it never be!"* in Romans 6. And the implications of this question pivot on our understanding of the word "sin" here. Does sin refer to an abstraction—namely, to acts of sin committed by the believer? Or does it refer to the totally depraved sin nature still in him or her?

# BREAKING IT DOWN

In the context of Romans 5:20-21, sin is personified as a reigning king: "Sin reigned in death." Here is the key then to the interpretation of the sixth chapter of Romans. Every time the word *sin* is used in this chapter as a noun, it refers to the sin nature. Read Romans 6 and in every instance where *sin* is mentioned (verses 1, 2, 6, 10, 11, 13, 14, 16, 17, 18, 20, 22, 23), replace it with *sinful nature.* Light will flood your understanding of Paul. In other words, there is a tremendous difference between unplanned occasional sin and sin that is habitual and continual because its source is derived from the sinful nature.

In its proper context then, verse one reads, "Shall we continue (habitually) to live in sin?" The Greek word translated *continue* is *menō*; it means to remain or abide and is used in the New Testament of a person abiding in someone's home as a guest or of a person abiding in a house. It implies fellowship, cordial relations, dependence, and social intercourse.

Replace *sin* with *sinful nature* and add the fuller context of *menō* in your reading and the interpretation of verse one is as follows:

> Shall we continue habitually to sustain the same relationship with the sinful nature that we sustained before we were saved, a relationship which was most cordial, a relationship in which we were fully yielded to and dependent upon that sinful nature, and all of this a habit of life?

# QUESTION ONE

With this proper context and understanding now before us, let us look at the first question asked in Romans 6:1: "What shall we say then? Are we to continue in sin so that grace might increase?" Verse two is Paul's knee-jerk reaction to this possibility: "God forbid!" or "May it never be!"

His second answer is more rational: "How shall we who died to sin (the sinful nature) still live in it?" He demonstrates that for a Christian to habitually sustain the same relationship to indwelling sin—a relationship characterized by a state of yieldedness to the sin, dependence on it, and cordiality with it—is a mechanical impossibility.

"How is that not possible?" someone might ask.

Paul's response in verses two through fourteen is straightforward: it's against our new nature to habitually yield to the evil nature. We are not persons of such a nature anymore.

## CHRISTIANS ARE NOT SUCCESSFUL SINNERS

I want to be clear, Paul answers the question in verse one of whether a Christian can habitually live in sin by declaring in verse two that it is a mechanical impossibility for a believer in Jesus Christ to live a life of habitual sin. In other words, once you have truly been born again, you will never be a successful sinner again. The person who has truly been born of God is not comfortable with habitual sin that continues for any length of time. Born-again believers cannot sin without the Holy Spirit convicting them, challenging them, and creating remorse within them. They cannot get away from the need for repentance! The most dangerous place for an individual to be in is for them to sin and not feel conviction anymore. This is the ultimate sign that the Holy Spirit's presence is not dwelling within them.

# THE DETHRONED MONARCH

In Romans 6:3, Paul describes the role of baptism in the process of dethroning the sin nature. The Greek word *baptizo* conveys the idea of introducing or placing a person or a thing in a new environment or into union with something else so as to alter its previous condition or its relationship to its previous environment.

In other words, God introduces the sinner into vital union with Jesus Christ in order that the sinful nature be broken and the divine nature implanted. Through his identification with Christ in His death, burial, and resurrection, the sinner's previous condition and his relationship to his previous environment is altered, bringing him into a new environment—the Kingdom of God.

The importance of baptism as participation in Christ's death is underscored pointedly by A.W. Tozer, who notes that "Among the plastic saints of our times Jesus has to do all the dying and all we want is to hear another sermon about His dying."[1]

In verses five and six, Paul emphasizes that God placed us into Christ when He died so that we might share His death and thus come into the benefits of that identification with Him, namely being separated from the sin nature as part of the salvation He confers when we believe. We have been placed into a new environment. The old nature was that of the first Adam, who made us sinners, heaping on condemnation. In our new environment in Christ, we have righteousness and life. We have moved from the condition of sinners who habitually and continually sin as a lifestyle to saints who can occasionally sin, but whose lifestyle is not one of habitual and continual sin by any means.

## UNDER THE KNIFE

In verses seven through nine, Paul demonstrates how we are not just placed in Christ to share His death to separate us from the sinful nature, but that we have also been placed in Him that we might share His resurrection and have His divine life imparted to us.

Earlier I called this process a surgical operation, and that is exactly what it is. We are disengaged and separated from the evil nature and are no longer compelled to obey it. Then the divine life is imparted, a new source of ethical, moral, and spiritual life which causes the believer to love righteousness and hate sin. It also empowers the believer with the desire and ability to do God's will.

"Carry this process of separation and impartation to its ultimate conclusion: your own salvation," admonishes Paul in Philippians 2:12-13 (paraphrased), "for God is the One who is constantly putting forth energy in you, giving you both the desire and the power to do IIis good pleasure."

Our will as believers has been completely set free. Before salvation it was not free so far as choosing between good and evil. Our will was enslaved to the sin nature. Now our will is free. It stands between the sin nature and the divine nature, with the responsibility to reject the sin nature. We don't need it and we are under no compulsion to plug back into it. When it becomes a habit to continually say "Yes" to the divine nature and "No" to the sin nature, we are walking in total victory over sin.

# QUESTION TWO

Paul identifies the second question in Romans 6:15: "What then? Shall we sin because we are not under law but under grace? May it never be!"

The second question presupposes a life of planned, infrequent, and spasmodic acts of sin, because grace makes it impossible to live a life of habitual sin. Paul answers this question in verses sixteen through twenty-three by showing that the Christian has changed masters. Where the Lord Jesus is master, it is not in his nature to sin.

Peter tells us that God has called us to be holy. "But just as He who called you is holy, so be holy in all you do, for it is written: 'Be holy because I am holy'" (1 Pet. 1:15-16 NIV).

In Romans 1:7 and First Corinthians 1:2, Paul greets believers in Rome and Corinth as those "called to be holy." He tells the Thessalonians that God did not call them to be impure, "but to live a holy life" (1 Thess. 4:7 NIV).

Paul underscores this later in First Thessalonians when he says, "God himself, the God of peace, sanctify you through and through," adding, "The one who calls you is faithful, and He will do it" (1 Thess. 5:23-24 NIV).

We have not only been called to be holy and live holy as believers, but this has been the plan of God for our lives from the beginning of time!

"He chose us in Him before the foundation of the world...[to] be holy and blameless before Him," Paul tells us in Ephesians 1:4.

To know and understand what God has called us to is of infinite importance in the life of a Christian.

## FREEDOM IN CHRIST

We have now discovered in Romans 6 that to Paul the apostle, using grace as a license to sin or even making provision for planned sin is absurd. This type of thinking is an assault on the blood of Jesus Christ that was shed at Calvary. We can have consistent victory over sin on a daily basis and walk in complete freedom and deliverance. We must continue to renew our minds and hide the Word of God deep down in our hearts that we might not sin against the Lord.

# PRAYER FOR DELIVERANCE

*Father, in Jesus' name, we tear down every paradigm and religious thought system that has exalted sin over the power of Your Son Jesus Christ. We say that all victory, power, and authority is found in the blood shed on the cross. We bind up addiction and lies that have made provision for any and all sin in our lives. We choose this day to walk according to the Holy Spirit and ask for great grace to be our portion. In the name that's above every name. Jesus Christ!*

## NOTE

1.  A.W. Tozer, *Man: The Dwelling Place of God* (Chicago, IL: Moody Publishers, 1997), 117.

*Chapter Eleven*

## BUILD MY HOUSE OF PRAYER

*I* remember the days after the visitation by the two angels in my hotel room like it was yesterday. I could not eat because I was so shaken at the thought of the deep, cleansing judgment I knew God would bring to His house before the glory many of us long for would manifest. As I wept on my floor, one question erupted from my heart and soul and it was this: "Father, what is the primary purpose of this cleansing judgment that is coming to Your House?"

He answered immediately, "So that My house might become a house of prayer once again. So that intimacy with Me might be prioritized far above ministry to people. So that a fresh fear of who I am might be manifested. So that mixture might be exposed and purity become a reality desired once again. So that My latter glory will far surpass the former."

## Cleansing the Temple

I'm convinced that before Jesus Christ returns for His Church, He is first coming to His Church. And as we have learned throughout this book, a major purpose of His coming to His Church is to bring His cleansing judgment. In the words of Peter, it is *time!*

It is time for us as saints and church leaders to agree and cry out for His cleansing. Without it, the latter glory will never come! Let us never forget that at the beginning of Jesus' public ministry, He cleansed the temple, and that toward the end of His public ministry, He cleansed it again! Twice! And after cleansing the temple, Jesus proclaims, "For My house shall become a house of prayer."

# A New Breed of Leader

In the years ahead, we will witness a tremendous shift in the house of God from the entertainment and pleasing of people into a realm of pure and simple-hearted devotion to Jesus Christ. This new breed of leader has been convinced that their greatest privilege in life is to minister and make intercession to the Lord. They have caught hold of their "heavenly calling" as Hebrews 3:1 states. These leaders will place more emphasis on the secret place than the public place.

These individuals will be more familiar with a prayer room than a playroom. They will be men and women who would rather minister to an audience of One than an audience of hundreds or thousands.

These days are critical for the body of Christ. No greater assignment and invitation is being released from the Father above than to behold the beauty of His Son Jesus and inquire of Him in His temple (see

Ps. 27:4). I see a generation of priestly prophetic voices who will give themselves to unceasing night and day prayer; it will be one of the greatest waves of refreshing that pastors and leaders have ever known.

A.W. Tozer once asked, "What would it be like if the four living creatures filled American pulpits every Sunday? What would they talk about?" These are the living creatures who have eyes in front and in back and who continually stand before the throne and behold the person of Jesus. I believe they would constantly and consistently testify to what Jesus is really like. They would not desire to speak of anything else.

What if a new breed of leaders and prophets, like the four living creatures, gave their entire ministries to beholding and giving testimony to Jesus? God the Father is restoring His true seers to His body. A commitment to the place of travail and intercession will mark church leadership in the days ahead as they become impregnated with the very purposes of God.

## CORPORATE PRAYER MEETINGS

As a leader in the body of Christ, I refuse to define success (fruit) among a community of believers outside the context of attendance at corporate prayer meetings. The early church in the book of Acts was birthed from a corporate prayer meeting (the upper room) and also sustained by corporate prayer meetings (house to house and the temple).

In the words of Leonard Ravenhill, "Sunday morning church attendance shows how popular the church is; Sunday night shows how popular the preacher is; and attendance at prayer meetings shows how popular God is."

We have many popular preachers and ministries in the earth, but a God in heaven who has largely been forgotten. We need to repent, but there are hardly any preachers and ministries calling saints to prayer meetings!

So long as prayer rooms are empty during the week while Sunday morning services are filled, we will never inherit the measure of glory God wants to pour out upon His house. Corporate prayer within the body of Christ is what is going to birth this next move of God. We simply cannot long for revival and glory and not want to pray!

## RAISING DEAD SONS AND DAUGHTERS

The story is told in First Kings 17:22 of God hearing the voice of Elijah the prophet as he cried out on behalf of the dead son of a widow lady. This is the first instance in the Bible of anyone being raised from the dead and as such is an invitation to receive revelation!

Elijah came in and carried the dead boy in his arms up into *the upper room* where he was staying (1 Kings 17:19-23).

What did Elijah understand in that moment that the widow mother did not?

Elijah knew that dead sons and daughters can only be raised from the dead from a place of prayer called *the upper room!* The widow mother had no power and authority to see her dead son raised from the dead because she failed to ascend into the upper room of prayer!

I want to encourage those reading this who have children who are not serving the Lord to take your children to the place of prayer called the upper room! Stop groaning over their lives and blaming yourself from a soulish realm and get into the place of prayer and ask God to raise them from the dead. Parents of prodigals, it is *time* to ascend to the Upper Room!

# THE HOLY AND PROFANE

As God's house becomes the true place of encounter and prayer that He intended for it to be, we will see a clear standard of righteousness drop like a plumb line in the Church. The same word of the Lord for the sons of Zadok will be spoken over those given the privilege of ministering before the Lord: "You shall teach My people the difference between the holy and the profane and cause them to discern between the unclean and clean."

In other words, those who minister to the Lord and spend hours in His presence will be best equipped to teach people discernment in the days ahead.

# A Charge to Church Leaders

We must refuse to "do ministry" apart from the place of intimacy with God. Our highest priority is not connecting with people; it is connecting with God. How can we effectively minister to people if we first do not learn how to minister to the Lord?

We must seek to spend long hours a week in the place of prayer and worship. We need to open up the Word of God and let Him pour out His Spirit upon us with fresh revelation and encounters. Mike Bickle correctly states, "The greatest disease in church leadership today is leaders who have no time for prayerful, long, and loving meditation on the Word of God and a lifestyle of prayer and fasting."

At corporate gatherings, the saints should honor fivefold ministry leaders who have learned how to kneel before God in the secret place before standing before men in the public place. A spirit of prayer and tangible fresh anointing of the Spirit should rest upon our spiritual leaders.

In ministry, God Himself is our greatest reward and highest prize. May the oil of intimacy and fresh revelation that only comes from long hours spent with Him mark this generation of fivefold ministry leaders.

# REVIVALISTS CONFRONT BOREDOM

God the Father is raising up and releasing a new breed of prophetic messengers and revivalists to the body of Christ that carry an express assignment to confront believers with their boredom with God.

These burning and shining lamps will cry out from behind the pulpits to the people of God like Jeremiah of old and declare, "What injustice did your fathers find in Me, that they went far from Me and walked after emptiness and became empty?" (Jer. 2:5). These heralds will be filled with the knowledge of God and be instrumentally used to restore awe and wonder to the body of Christ. I prophesy that the gift of repentance and oil of intimacy will mark the ministries of these revivalists and prophetic messengers. In essence, their calling and message to God's people can be summed up in three words: "Return to Me!" says the Lord.

Be on the lookout for fascinated messengers who continually live from the throne room and behold the beauty of Jesus, crying out and confronting a generation bored with God who continually live from the entertainment room beholding the carnality of man.

## THE GLORY TO COME

Vance Havner once said, "Revival is simply New Testament Christianity. It's the saints getting back to normal."

In the book of Acts, the supernatural becomes normalized. The saints didn't know anything other than signs, wonders, and miracles on a daily basis. In my visitation in the hotel room in California, the cleansing angel told me that there was a "boom that would come to the upper room," but first there had to come the "broom," representing the cleansing.

In Acts 2, at Pentecost we see a type of "boom" where men begin to speak in other languages. Peter declares this is part of the fulfillment of the second chapter of Joel.

Could there be another "boom in the upper room" like the angel said?

Could there be spontaneous booms all over the earth?

I emphatically believe the answer is "Yes!"

# THE EMERGENCE OF HOUSE GATHERINGS

I believe the glory that is coming to the Church as we embrace the cleansing judgment is going to be primarily hosted in homes across the earth. The incense that will rise as the house of God shifts back to a primary focus of ministry to Yahweh will come from neighborhoods and rural communities all over the world. Small and intimate settings will not be able to measure the kind of glory that is coming. Entire neighborhoods will be won to Jesus Christ in a day as the sick are healed, devils are cast out, and regions are won for the glory of God. It is going to be spectacular.

### *The Three Cord Strand*

As I pressed in to the Lord about what the DNA will be for these houses that will contain His glory in the days ahead, He specifically spoke to me about three realities:

- Fire

- Family
- Fathering

The fire of God was always meant to be stewarded in the context of a spiritual family with the oversight and care of fathers of the faith. Where there is fire (zeal, passion, love) for Jesus among spiritual families (of all ages) with the protection and oversight of spiritual fathers, there will be a glory abiding upon the house of God that we have never seen before. The depth of love between the generations will be noticed by those in the world around us. Pure, simple-hearted devotion to Jesus Christ will mark our gatherings. Fathering will heal the many wounds of hurting sons and daughters who do not know how to trust anymore or crave platforms because of the multitude of their insecurities.

Imagine with me now, the cleansing judgment of the Lord falling upon His house all over the earth. Exposure, purification, repentance, and a healthy, holy fear of God is restored to the Church.

And then?

Pure glory!

The return to our first love will drench the global Church with the beautiful fragrance of Christ! The supernatural becomes normal because we have learned that all true spiritual authority is born from intimacy with God. House meetings explode all over the earth where fire, family, and fathers become the wineskin that will hold a true last-days outpouring of the Holy Spirit.

Saints, there is glory coming!

As we see these days approach, let us turn inwardly to the Father and ask the Holy Spirit to search our hearts. May the end-time Church in personal and corporate agreement pray with David: "Search me and know me, oh God; find any offensive way in me and lead me down the path everlasting!"

Only then can the Holy Spirit begin His work of revealing truth that will lead us into a lifestyle of continual intimacy, power, and glory.

The need has never been greater!

Even so, Maranatha! Lord Jesus, come!

# AFTERWORD

*C*learly, Scripture prophesizes a great outpouring of the Spirit to precede the return of the Lord. In Isaiah 60:1-3, God promised, "Arise, shine; for your light has come, and the glory of the Lord has risen upon you. For behold, darkness will cover the earth and deep darkness the peoples; but the Lord will rise upon you and His glory will appear upon you. Nations will come to your light, and kings to the brightness of your rising." You might assume that this applied only to ancient Israel returning from Babylonian exile, but I submit that it never really happened for literal Israel. It's a prophecy for God's people, Jews and Gentiles who have received Messiah Jesus, who will walk in glory together in the midst of the gathering darkness of the last days.

Joel prophesied similarly in Joel 2:28-31, a promise only partly fulfilled on the Day of Pentecost. "It will come about after this that I will pour out My Spirit on all mankind; and your sons and daughters will prophesy, your old men will dream dreams, your young men will see visions. Even on the male and female servants I will pour out My Spirit in those days. I will display wonders in the sky and on the earth, blood, fire and columns of smoke. The sun will be turned into darkness and the moon into blood before the great and awesome day of the Lord comes." Peter declared this fulfilled in his sermon in Acts 2—and it was certainly one fulfillment, a foreshadowing—but the fullness of Joel's prophecy is yet to come.

Finally, looking to our future, Revelation 7:9-10 says, "After these things I looked, and behold, a great multitude which no one could count, from every nation and all tribes and peoples and tongues, standing before the throne and before the Lamb, clothed in white robes, and palm branches were in their hands; and they cry out with a loud voice, saying, 'Salvation to our God who sits on the throne, and to the Lamb.'" Surely, John envisioned the great end-time harvest, the result of a great end-time outpouring of God's Holy Spirit.

Never does God act without first revealing His secret counsel to His servants, the prophets (see Amos 3:7). Any great move of God will therefore be announced by forerunners sent to prepare the way and ready God's people to receive what He intends to do. Before the ministry of Jesus would begin, the Father sent John the Baptist to announce the coming of the kingdom and to cry out for the people to prepare. "Repent, for the kingdom of heaven is at hand" (Matt. 3:2). He preached in fulfillment of Isaiah's prophecy that one would come to call people to prepare the way of the Lord and make His paths straight.

In the Ancient Near East, roads were maintained only when the king intended a visit. Messengers went before him to tell the people to smooth the road, to take out the rocks and the obstacles. When God plans a great outpouring, He sends His messengers to proclaim, as John the Baptist did, a message of repentance in order that the Spirit of God will have a solid and unobstructed pathway on which to travel. John the Baptist warned that the King was coming and called for repentance to prepare His highway in the hearts of men and women.

Today, as then, God is sending a company of John the Baptist prophets to proclaim a last-days outpouring of the Holy Spirit that will fulfill the whole of Joel's prophecy and eclipse even the Day of Pentecost in power and scope. While still very small in number, these messengers cry for repentance and holiness with an urgency born of passion and hunger, both for the presence of the Lord and for the welfare of God's people.

The holiness for which they long is not laced with a list of rules to obey, but points rather to conformity to the image of the Son of God. Far from being a prison of legalism and condemnation, their message calls for transformation that flows from true union with Jesus. Rather than working from outward behavior to inward holiness, which never bears the true fruit of love, it works from inward transformation that issues in righteous behavior, free from the destruction sin brings. Real holiness has never been focused on the list of things we must not do, but is rather about the wonderful things we're freed to become.

Let the John the Baptist prophets arise and let their voices be heard in the land. Let an awakening come upon God's people. Let our ways of heart, mind and soul that fail to conform to the image of our Lord be exposed and cleansed. Let transformation come and let a generation of the righteous come forth whose light draws the nations to the Lord we serve.

R. LOREN SANDFORD
New Song Church and Ministries

# ABOUT JEREMIAH JOHNSON

Jeremiah Johnson planted and is the apostolic overseer of Heart of the Father Ministry in Lakeland, Florida. A bestselling author and globally recognized prophet, Jeremiah travels extensively throughout the United States and abroad as a conference and guest speaker. He is the host of his own television show called *The Watchman's Corner* which airs on the PTL network every week. Jeremiah has also been a guest on Christian television and radio shows including *The Jim Bakker Show*, Sid Roth's *It's Supernatural!*, and *The Line of Fire* with Dr. Michael Brown, as well as on networks such as Daystar, TBN, and God TV. Jeremiah and his wife reside in Florida with their four children.

For more information,
please visit www.jeremiahjohnson.tv.